"WHO AM I?"
The Loss Human Factor
Volume 3

The Power
of
Knowing Thyself

PAA KWASI MFOAMFO

The Power of Knowing Thyself

The Loss Human Factor, Volume 3

Paa Kwasi Mfoamfo

Published by Paa Kwasi Mfoamfo, 2024.

Table of Contents

Dedication

To the countless individuals on this planet Earth, it is my utmost desire that you discover your real selves, so that you do not become generational thieves, robbing us of your value to this world.

To you, the reader, I convince that the reason you may have this book at this time in your life reading is that, you know there is a person trapped on the inside of you, streaming to be released, struggling under a culture that does not believe in you. This book has come for you to have the first-ever encounter with yourself, to expose the truth you already know that is buried within you, that will set you free from the lies they told you about yourself.

Acknowledgement

A tragedy would have unfolded, leading to the death of this book within me, were it not for the enduring impact of both living individuals and those who have passed but continue to shape my life from beyond their graveyards. Their unleashed potentials, too numerous to capture within the constraints of time, have played an important role in the creation of this book. I express heartfelt gratitude for channeling this book from within me with your inherent abilities and resources. May your influence persist, transcending the boundaries of time, and may you endure until the moment when time interrupts eternity. Thank you sincerely.

Table Of Contents

Preface

"The worth of a book is not determined by the author or its price, but by how much wisdom it draws out from within you, exposing aspects of yourself you never knew existed."—Paa Kwasi Mfoamfo

From the moment we enter this world, we are labelled with a name, assigned a religion, tagged with a nationality, and categorized by race. These markers shape our view of ourselves, confining us to a narrow identity that dictates our existence.

Put simply, our surroundings and upbringing often do not encourage us to explore who we truly are. Many of us grow up in environments where our inherent potential is not nurtured, and instead, we are molded to fit into a predefined cultural identity. This process starts from birth, making it difficult for us to distinguish our own identities. Consequently, we often try to define ourselves through external factors such as religion, social affiliations, jobs, and achievements. This struggle with self-identity leads many to emulate others and conform to societal norms, rather than embracing their uniqueness.

The result is a world filled with individuals who lack a strong sense of self. Instead of standing out, many blend into the crowd, adopting the identities of others in an attempt to feel important. This explains why trends and fashions hold such sway over us – they provide a sense of other identities when our own identities are unclear.

The key to breaking free from this cycle lies in rediscovering our true selves. We must strive to reclaim the essence of who we are, so that others can identified us before in pack of humanity. This means moving away from the "one-size-fits-all" mentality and embracing the unique gifts trapped on the inside of us that make us who we are. Only then can we truly answer the question, "Who am I?" and carve out our own path in life.

So, the next time someone calls your name, consider what they see in you. Are you just another face in the crowd, or do you stand out for your authentic self?

The human question—"Who am I?" is simple yet complex because we can be very assuming that we know the answer until our assumptions are stripped away and our ignorance is exposed. This question haunts all of us, and the reality is that we do not talk about it at all because we want people to believe we have the answer. We also do not discuss it too often because we are afraid we cannot answer, yet our lives are made up of this question: "Who am I?"

Who are you? It is not a question about your name, ethnicity, tribe, nation, continent, position, profession, job title, social status, nor your life's current condition or biological orientations.

In order to answer this question, you must begin with these phrase: "I am..." In fact, we do not even use these phrase at all because our cultural environment does not code for self-discovery. Once you claim that you know who you are, there is an immediate reaction, and all hell breaks loose on you because society knows you are not supposed to know it without their information and validation.

In today's world, religion often shapes our sense of identity. It acts as a registry, telling us who we are and validating it. This mirrors the prejudices among religious groups today, who, despite claiming modernity, still seek conversions and struggle to accept the identity of those outside their faith. This leads to assumptions about people based on their religion, often escalating to hatred, violence, and even wars, much like how the Pharisees questioned Jesus for not aligning with their religious views, as well as other groups like the Sadducees and Herodians. Essentially, they sought to confine His identity within the bounds of religion, similarly to how many of us grapple with religious identities imposed upon us rather than finding our own sense of self.

Friend, all that you are seeking for in life is already in existence, waiting for you to embrace it. The paradox is you do not have to seek it first; seek the thyself trapped within yourself first, and all other things you need in life will be attracted to you.

I wonder what is trapped within you, just like there is flight trapped in every bird, swim in every fish, forest of trees in every seed. A seed is not really a seed; that is a fact. And what is a fact? A fact is the present description of the state of a thing. And what is the truth? It is a forest of trees, thus what it really is. So next time you have a mango seed in your palm, the truth is you are having an entire forest of trees in your palm, but the fact is, it is just a seed. Never once in your life confuse facts with truths. A fact is the description of the present state of a thing, and truth is what really a thing is. Let me guide you through the pages of this book, where you will have your first-ever encounter with the truth you already know that is buried within you, that will set you free from the lies they told you about yourself.

Chapter

1

The Greatest Common Desire of All Humans

"Most of the trouble in the world is caused by people wanting to be important."—T.S Eliot

The most deadly silent pain is the pain of being ignored. I believe that all humans have experienced this kind of pain to some degree or another because our greatest common desire in life is the desire to feel important. This desire is not just common, it is the greatest of all desires. Every person on Earth has an inherent desire to feel important, to feel significant and valued. This desire is an absolute need of human existence; often when unacknowledged, it is deeply felt. We all long to know that we matter, that we hold worth and are considered special. It is an utmost need we are driven by, yet many deny its significance. Our pursuit of feeling valuable and respected drives us to great lengths, sometimes engaging in unusual behaviors. This greatest desire for importance leads us to dress provocatively, alter our appearances in unconventional ways, or even adorn ourselves with extravagant items to stand out, even with our sweat and blood from our lower incomes.

This greatest desire is profound and touches upon our core need for recognition. That is why being ignored cuts deeply, causing emotional pain that most have experienced at some point. How does it feel when your heartfelt words are ignored or when someone dearest to you disregards you? The sting of being overlooked or dismissed affects us all. Being sidelined in a conversation, not receiving eye contact, or being excluded leaves a profound impact because we crave acknowledgment. Rejection, whether subtle or overt, triggers feelings of unworthiness and silent depression. The feeling of unimportance extends beyond personal interactions. It seeps into how our emotions are disregarded or our hardships go unnoticed. The absence of validation, appreciation, and reassurance leaves a void, making us silently question our importance. Even the fluctuation in social media attention can deeply affect our sense of importance, as we yearn for validation through subscribers, followers, likes, comments, reviews, and shares.

In its effect, the greatest common human desire for importance is a fundamental drive that influences our actions and emotions. It governs our pursuit of recognition and value, affecting us in various aspects of life, from personal interactions to our presence in the digital world.

The tragic aspect is that our desire to feel important is the greatest threat to our human civilization. People no longer know themselves, so they do not know what they ought to develop into; instead, they develop into something unnatural, to the extreme of changing their reproductive systems, the natural human preference for the opposite sex, and even sell their bodies on the streets and on the media. Others are involved in gangs shooting each other to gain access to wealth and hoard it to feel significant.

Additionally, some rely entirely on the fashion industry; hence, it is not surprising to see someone dressed in a combination of attractive colors, while others appear almost naked, whether in the media or at social gatherings. It is also not surprising for people to style their hair in unusual ways or undergo surgery to attain what they call a "Coca-Cola bottle" shape. Why would people do everything they can to live on the cutting edge of technology, purchasing the latest trending brands? Moreover, some people manipulate others to gain positions of power, even sacrificing other people's lives, including those of their own relatives, to succeed in life and be noticed. The desire to feel important is the deepest motivation in our world today.

PEOPLE ARE NOT SEEKING YOU OUT

Millions of individuals have lived entire lifetimes much like Methuselah, who, according to the Bible, lived for an astonishing nine hundred and sixty-nine years on our small speck in the vast universe known as planet Earth. Despite their existence, they went largely unnoticed by humanity. They were laid to rest in graves, and until now, their presence remained unknown to us except for the markers on their graves. It is conceivable that one hundred and fifty years from today, none of us currently reading this or whether listening to this on a tape will still be alive.

If we take a journey back one hundred and fifty years before our time, none of those who shouldered the burdens of the world then would still be with us today. Why do we remember some people while forgetting others entirely? Often, the only remembrance we have of certain individuals is the inscription on their tombstones.

This brings to mind the idea that people are not seeking you out specifically; rather, they are interested in what is trapped on the inside of you. If you fail to showcase what you possess, the world will simply ignore you. Just being present on this planet does not guarantee that others will take notice of you.

In simpler terms, the world connects with your presence and also senses your absence based on your self-deployment. Let us think of it like this: imagine you are an apple seed. If you do not grow into an apple tree and produce fruit, people might not see your worth. They might step on you, throw rubbish at you, disqualify you for certain things, lay you off, reduce you to nothing or even rain insult on you because they do not understand your potential to nourish them, contribute to the landscape of the environment, and your economic importance as well. However, a few people might see beyond what it is and recognize what you should and could be. So, the real essence of an apple seed is not the seed itself, but the fruit it is meant to grow into.

That is why I am convinced that your number one greatest common goal in life should be self-deployment rather than self-importance. Why am I saying this? Because people cannot ignore that which they know the value of. And self-deployment entails that there is a gift trapped in you that you were meant to deliver to this generation and the succeeding ones, which made your birth necessary to exist on the planet Earth at this moment in history. And your value in life in this world is the gift you were meant to deliver to humanity.

Gift is the inherent potential that serves a purpose, fulfilling a need in creation. That means everybody has a gift within him or her, specifically to solve a problem in this world, and that means that no human on Earth is a biological accident of sperm and egg. We show up on this planet not just to suck up oxygen; there is a reason for our presence. All of us, an untold number of humans on this planet Earth, were born with the seed of a solution to a problem, and that solution is natural within us. And one's value in life comes from the problem he or she uses his or her gift to solve; that is why if one does not feel valuable or important to his or her generation and the world, it could be that the individual has not yet discovered their gift and does not know their function or the part they were destined to play in this world. If humanity would understand this simple revelation, no one would even consider sacrificing his or her life on the altar of suicide.

The paradox here is: being born with a gift trapped on the inside of each and every one of us, including the one sleeping under a bridge on a cardboard, the one sitting on the floor begging for something, the one receiving high payment and living a luxury life, the one confined within the four walls of a prison cell, and the one stuck on a hospital bed, does not mean we are going to be noticed by everyone and be valuable to the world.

The greatest ticket to being IMPORTANT, OR VALUABLE

The greatest ticket to being valuable to humanity lies behind the gift you serve to humanity. Your value in life comes from the gift you were born to deliver to this world. So, if you never discover the gift you were meant to deliver to this world, you will never be valuable to us. Because your gift is more important than you are, and it is what makes you valuable, as you carry it within. That is to tell that, the extent to which our presence and absence will be felt depends on the number of problems we solve using our inherent gifts.

Behind every act of service lies an element of greatness. Your potential for greatness resides in the specific gift you were born to offer humanity. If success and wealth are our aspirations, then serving others through our gifts should be our top most priority in life as well as our greatest motivation.

Within every individual on this planet Earth resides an untapped wealth of potential solutions meant to be released. Each person bears the seed of their potential for greatness, locked within the gift they have to offer humanity. Failing to share this gift means never realizing one's potential for greatness, as well as never being noticed by humanity.

Buried in the quiet grounds of the graveyard

In every generation, there are individuals who hold the answers to the questions that trouble society. These people possess unique gifts that can save humanity from its daily crises. Unfortunately, many individuals pass away without ever knowing they are saviours of solving the specific issue they were meant to tackle. This leads me to believe that the most completely developed, haven, wealthiest and valuable place on Earth is not a bustling city or a thriving marketplace, but rather the quiet grounds of the graveyard. Within these solemn grounds lie untapped treasures - gifts that were never unleashed to confront the everyday problems plaguing our world.

Among the buried gifts are potentially groundbreaking industrial enterprises worth billions, life-saving medical breakthroughs, revolutionary economic theories capable of resolving global crises, visionary government policies, influential charitable organizations, ingenious inventions, captivating television shows, films, songs, poems, motivational speeches, educational textbooks, inspiring sermons, nutritious recipes, skilled artists who will create meaningful paintings and sculptures, insightful historians who will illuminate our past to guide our present and future, comedians who will bring joy and solace to troubled souls, and countless other gifts. It is these gifts that hold the key to solving humanity's most pressing issues and ensuring the proper functioning of our world.

Our gifts are the solutions that humanity desperately needs in order to thrive. It is through the utilization of our unique gifts that the world can be saved from its challenges and function optimally. Therefore, it is essential for each individual to re-understand the purpose and power of their life—(I talked about this topic in more detail, which I believe is the source of all our individual and social ills in my book titled *"Why*

Am I Here?" of The Lost Human Factor, Volume 2. Please, I urge you to get a copy of this book so that you can enhance your understanding of your importance to our world and realize that you are needed by humanity),—and contribute their gifts to the betterment of the world. Only then can we truly create a world where everyone can flourish.

PRINCIPLES WORTH REMEMBERING

1. The most deadly silent pain is the pain of being ignored. I believe that all humans have experienced this kind of pain to some degree or another because our greatest common desire in life is the desire to feel important. This desire is an absolute need of human existence; often when unacknowledged, it is deeply felt.

2. How does it feel when your heartfelt words are ignored or when someone dearest to you disregards you? The sting of being overlooked or dismissed affects us all. Being sidelined in a conversation, not receiving eye contact, or being excluded leaves a profound impact because we crave acknowledgment. Rejection, whether subtle or overt, triggers feelings of unworthiness and silent depression. The feeling of unimportance extends beyond personal interactions. It seeps into how our emotions are disregarded or our hardships go unnoticed. The absence of validation, appreciation, and reassurance leaves a void, making us silently question our importance. Even the fluctuation in social media attention can deeply affect our sense of importance, as we yearn for validation through subscribers, followers, likes, comments, reviews, and shares.

3. People are not seeking you out specifically; rather, they are interested in what is trapped on the inside of you. If you fail to showcase what you possess, the world will simply ignore you. Just being present on this planet does not guarantee that others will take notice of you.

4. I am convinced that your number one greatest common goal in life should be self-deployment rather than self-importance.

Why am I saying this? Because people cannot ignore that which they know the value of. And self-deployment entails that there is a gift trapped in you that you were meant to deliver to this generation and the succeeding ones, which made your birth necessary to exist on the planet Earth at this moment in history.

5. *Gift is the inherent potential that serves a purpose, fulfilling a need in creation.*

6. No human on Earth is a biological accident of sperm and egg. We show up on this planet not just to suck up oxygen; there is a reason for our presence. All of us, an untold number of humans on this planet Earth, were born with the seed of a solution to a problem, and that solution is natural within us. And one's value in life comes from the problem he or she uses his or her gift to solve; that is why if one does not feel valuable or important to his or her generation and the world, it could be that the individual has not yet discovered their gift and does not know their function or the part they were destined to play in this world. If humanity would understand this simple revelation, no one would even consider sacrificing his or her life on the altar of suicide.

7. The greatest ticket to being valuable to humanity lies behind the gift you serve to humanity. Your value in life comes from the gift you were born to deliver to this world. So, if you never discover the gift you were meant to deliver to this world, you will never be valuable to us.

8. Behind every act of service lies an element of greatness. Your potential for greatness resides in the specific gift you were born to offer humanity. If success and wealth are our aspirations, then serving others through our gifts should be our top most priority in life as well as our greatest motivation.

9. Within every individual on this planet Earth resides an untapped wealth of potential solutions meant to be released.

Each person bears the seed of their potential for greatness, locked within the gift they have to offer humanity. Failing to share this gift means never realizing one's potential for greatness, as well as never being noticed by humanity.

10. In every generation, there are individuals who hold the answers to the questions that trouble society. These people possess unique gifts that can save humanity from its daily crises. Unfortunately, many individuals pass away without ever knowing they are saviours of solving the specific issue they were meant to tackle. This leads me to believe that the most completely developed, haven, wealthiest and valuable place on Earth is not a bustling city or a thriving marketplace, but rather the quiet grounds of the graveyard. Within these solemn grounds lie untapped treasures - gifts that were never unleashed to confront the everyday problems plaguing our world.

Chapter

2

Identity Conversion

"We're all God in disguise. Jesus found that out, and they crucified him for saying so."—Alan Watts

In this present era, many struggle to truly know themselves. Our identity seems elusive, leading us to seek different personas, yet we are uncertain about who we really are. Ironically, we are addicted to this pursuit without understanding our authentic selves, which poses a significant problem. The tragic loss of our human identity has deeply affected every aspect of our existence.

Cloaked in the allure of materialism, many have surrendered the essence of their identity to the garments they adorn. The once simple act of getting dressed has metamorphosed into a means of projecting an image, often one that aligns with societal expectations or conforms to fleeting trends. In this pursuit, the very core of selfhood is overshadowed by the external facade, leaving individuals adrift in a sea of superficiality.

A disconcerting subset of this phenomenon is the rise of dressing in sexually provocative manners. In a bid to gain attention or validation, individuals resort to using their bodies as canvases for societal approval. The tragic irony lies in the fact that the quest for identity through provocative attire often results in a commodification of the self, reducing one's essence to a mere object of sexual gratification.

Parallel to this, a pervasive desire to surround oneself with the wealthiest and elite has taken root. The pursuit of identity through association with affluence not only perpetuates social hierarchies but also fosters a culture where one's worth is measured by the company they keep. In this relentless pursuit of status, the authentic self becomes obscured, replaced by a carefully curated persona designed to fit seamlessly into exclusive circles.

In an age dominated by technology, the digital realm becomes a breeding ground for identity manipulation. The advent of AI-driven photo-editing applications has enabled individuals to sculpt their outward appearance, distorting reality to conform to societal ideals of beauty. The tragic loss of authenticity unfolds as faces are morphed into unattainable perfection, eroding the very essence of individuality.

Money, often revered as a means to an end, paradoxically becomes an end in itself for some. The pursuit of wealth as a primary source of identity can lead to a dehumanizing existence, where individuals are reduced to the sum of their financial achievements. The tragic consequence is a society that measures success solely in monetary terms, neglecting the richness of human experience that extends beyond the confines of wealth accumulation.

Beyond material pursuits, the quest for identity extends to the formation of social clubs and communities. While finding belonging is a fundamental human need, the tragic loss occurs when identity becomes synonymous with affiliation. Whether it be LGBTQIA+ groups, religious faith communities, or exclusive social clubs, the danger lies in individuals deriving their entire sense of self from external affiliations.

the most devastating experience that could happen to any human alive on this planet Earth

The cruelest thing that can happen to any human is not death, it is losing one's sense of self. This is the most devastating experience that could happen to any human alive on this planet Earth. This devastating experience leads individuals to disregard their own worth, often feeling unworthy and sacrificing their lives on the altar of a sense of purposelessness. The belief that their existence holds no significance to themselves or succeeding generations drives them towards a painful feeling of aimlessness, severing their ability to genuinely connect with others. Consequently, they become susceptible to manipulation, their weak self-perception rendering them easily influenced.

Many choose to retreat from social engagements, avoiding situations that challenge or question their identity. Some grapple with a sense of being fraudulent, incapable of embracing their life's purpose and achievements. Others attempt to evade reality's harshness by indulging in fleeting pleasures, only to find themselves mired in escapism.

The repercussions of this loss extend beyond the psychological realm, manifesting as stress-induced health complications arising from internal conflicts. Moreover, it extinguishes the once vibrant flames of motivation and passion, leaving individuals bereft of the drive to live effectively.

The absence of a sense of self forcefully steers some individuals towards perceiving themselves either inferior or superior to others. This unsettling loss might even propel them to alter their physical appearance drastically, adopting forms akin to animals. Some resort to unconventional sexual practices, seeking solace in intimate relationships with animals, same-sex partners, or artificial companions like sex machinery, toys, or dolls.

Furthermore, amidst this turmoil, there emerges a paradoxical reverence for fellow humans. Some elevate their peers to godlike status—worshipping them. And also worshipping created things in place of acknowledging God's assignment described in Genesis 1:26, where humanity was entrusted with dominion over all creation excluding fellow humans. This convoluted redefinition of self and reality compounds the agony of losing one's sense of identity, making it an unparalleled tragedy in the human experience.

No human knows you better than yourself

From the moment we enter this world, we are labelled with a name, assigned a religion, tagged with a nationality, and categorized by race. These markers shape our view of ourselves, confining us to a narrow identity that dictates our existence.

Put simply, our surroundings and upbringing often do not encourage us to explore who we truly are. Many of us grow up in environments where our inherent potential is not nurtured, and instead, we are molded to fit into a predefined cultural identity. This process starts from birth, making it difficult for us to distinguish our own identities. Consequently, we often try to define ourselves through external factors such as religion, social affiliations, jobs, and achievements. This struggle with self-identity leads many to emulate others and conform to societal norms, rather than embracing their uniqueness.

The result is a world filled with individuals who lack a strong sense of self. Instead of standing out, many blend into the crowd, adopting the identities of others in an attempt to feel important. This explains why trends and fashions hold such sway over us – they provide a sense of other identities when our own identities are unclear.

The key to breaking free from this cycle lies in rediscovering our true selves. We must strive to reclaim the essence of who we are, so that others can identified us before in pack of humanity. This means moving away from the "one-size-fits-all" mentality and embracing the unique gifts trapped on the inside of us that make us who we are. Only then can we truly answer the question, "Who am I?" and carve out our own path in life.

So, the next time someone calls your name, consider what they see in you. Are you just another face in the crowd, or do you stand out for your authentic self?

The most MISUNDERSTOOD human question—"Who am I?"

This question is simple yet complex because we can be very assuming that we know the answer until our assumptions are stripped away and our ignorance is exposed. This question haunts all of us, and the reality is that we do not talk about it at all because we want people to believe we have the answer. We also do not discuss it too often because we are afraid we cannot answer, yet our lives are made up of this question: "Who am I?"

Who are you? It is not a question about your name, ethnicity, tribe, nation, continent, position, profession, job title, social status, nor your life's current condition or biological orientations.

In order to answer this question, you must begin with these phrase: "I am..." then fill in the blank. I am much convinced there is no one on Earth in the history of humanity who has used these phrase "I am" more often than Jesus, and that is a revelation to us all that He knew who He really was. In fact, we do not even use these phrase at all because our cultural environment does not code for self-discovery. Once you claim that you know who you are, there is an immediate reaction, and all hell breaks loose on you because society knows you are not supposed to know it without their information and validation.

In the book of John in the New Testament of the Bible, as we are about to carefully read some of Jesus Christ's statements on His claim of who He really was and humanity's reactions to them, you would finally come into agreement with yourself and me on why we cannot use these phrase "I am..." more often than Jesus:

> *"I am the bread of life... For I have come down from Heaven..." (John 6:35, 38). "At this, the Jews began to grumble about Him because He said, 'I am the bread that came down from Heaven.' They said, 'Is this not Jesus, the son of Joseph, whose father and mother we know? How can He now say, 'I came down from Heaven'?" (John 6:41-42).*

"I am the light of the world. Whoever follows Me will never walk in darkness but will have the light of life" (John 8:12). "The Pharisees, therefore, said to Him, 'You bear witness of Yourself; Your witness is not true [valid]'" (John 8:13).

"I am the gate; whoever enters through Me will be saved... I am the good shepherd..." (John 10:9, 11). "At these words, the Jews were again divided. Many of them said, 'He is demon-possessed and raving mad. Why listen to him?'" (John 10:19-20).

"I and the Father are one. Then the Jews took up stones again to stone Him, but Jesus said to them, 'I have shown you many great miracles from the Father. For which of these do you stone Me?' 'We are not stoning You for any of these,' replied the Jews, 'but for blasphemy because You, a mere man, claim to be God.' Jesus answered them, 'Is it not written in your Law, 'I have said you are gods'? If He called them 'gods,' to whom the word of God came—and the Scripture cannot be broken—what about the one whom the Father set apart as His very own and sent into the world? Why then do you accuse Me of blasphemy because I said, 'I am God's Son'?" (John 10:30-36).

When looking closely, you will notice that every time Jesus claimed "I am...", there was a reaction. Firstly, they tried to define Him solely by His family and birthplace, much like many of us often let our upbringing define who we are. His second claim faced strong opposition from one of the most influential, powerful, and largest religious groups of His time, the Pharisees.

In today's world, religion often shapes our sense of identity. It acts as a registry, telling us who we are and validating it. During Jesus' era, He was questioned about the source and validity of His identity claims. This mirrors the prejudices among religious groups today, who, despite claiming modernity, still seek conversions and struggle to accept the identity of those outside their faith. This leads to assumptions about people based on their religion, often escalating to hatred, violence, and even wars, much like how the Pharisees questioned Jesus for not aligning with their religious views, as well as other groups like the Sadducees and Herodians. Essentially, they sought to confine His identity within the bounds of religion, similarly to how many of us grapple with religious identities imposed upon us rather than finding our own sense of self.

When they realized that Jesus was not merely an activist for show but actually embodied whoever He claimed to be, and that all the systems set in place could not convert His identity and made Him one of them, they forced to clone Him with one. They said, "He is demon-possessed and raving mad." This should remind us that no matter what we claim to be in the world, others have already formed opinions about who they think we are in their minds. If we deviate from their expectations, they may perceive us as out of touch with reality of their world and accuse us of creating illusions. Like Jesus, we should be prepared to handle these words that often come out of people's mouths, labeling us as "raving mad."

Friend, once people recognize that you are not just putting on a show as an activist and that you truly know and embody yourself, unable to be duplicated with other versions of yourself anymore, they start treating you with suspicion. Why? Simply because the very essence of being original bothers people. If you need a clear indicator that you are not just a replica of others, it is when you tend to annoy people. This demonstrates that you are not trying to prove you are different, but rather you are authentically expressing yourself, which inherently differs from the identity of others. Going through such turmoil in your life is akin to the experiences of Jesus, indicating that you truly understand and embody your identity.

This parallels with the last scripture verse, suggesting that being authentic and not a mere imitation strongly irritates people to the extent that they may even seek to harm you. Some individuals have even been killed for refusing to conform to the false identities society has imposed upon them, realizing that such conformity is not natural, unlike embracing one's true self. Being coerced into adopting another persona comes with a myriad of demands, rituals, and meeting certain expectations.

PRINCIPLES WORTH REMEMBERING

1. Cloaked in the allure of materialism, many have surrendered the essence of their identity to the garments they adorn. The once simple act of getting dressed has metamorphosed into a means of projecting an image, often one that aligns with societal expectations or conforms to fleeting trends. In this pursuit, the very core of selfhood is overshadowed by the external facade, leaving individuals adrift in a sea of superficiality.

2. In a bid to gain attention or validation, individuals resort to using their bodies as canvases for societal approval. The tragic irony lies in the fact that the quest for identity through provocative attire often results in a commodification of the self, reducing one's essence to a mere object of sexual gratification.

3. A pervasive desire to surround oneself with the wealthiest and elite has taken root. The pursuit of identity through association with affluence not only perpetuates social hierarchies but also fosters a culture where one's worth is measured by the company they keep. In this relentless pursuit of status, the authentic self becomes obscured, replaced by a carefully curated persona designed to fit seamlessly into exclusive circles.

4. In an age dominated by technology, the digital realm becomes a breeding ground for identity manipulation. The advent of AI-driven photo-editing applications has enabled individuals to sculpt their outward appearance, distorting reality to conform to societal ideals of beauty. The tragic loss of authenticity unfolds as faces are morphed into unattainable perfection, eroding the very essence of individuality.

5. The cruelest thing that can happen to any human is not death, it is losing one's sense of self. This is the most devastating

experience that could happen to any human alive on this planet Earth. This devastating experience leads individuals to disregard their own worth, often feeling unworthy and sacrificing their lives on the altar of a sense of purposelessness. The belief that their existence holds no significance to themselves or succeeding generations drives them towards a painful feeling of aimlessness, severing their ability to genuinely connect with others. Consequently, they become susceptible to manipulation, their weak self-perception rendering them easily influenced.

CHAPTER

3

Shifting Your Paradigm

"The first duty of a man is to think for himself."—José Martí

From the moment of our creation within the secure confines of our mother's womb, to our emergence as innocent beings onto this vast and complex Earth, we were like blank canvases, unaware of the intricate tapestry that lay before us. Our minds, like empty computer hard drives, knew nothing of the world and its wonders. Yet, as we grew and developed, certain concepts were introduced to us, woven into the fabric of our very beings through the gateways of our senses.

Our caregivers, our family, the influences of culture, education, religion, and scientific theories all played their part in shaping our belief systems. These various elements planted seeds of experience which gives us knowledge within the fertile soil of our hearts. Over time, these seeds transformed into belief systems that would guide our perception and reaction of reality.

One of the most influential factors in shaping our belief system is personal experience. Through the trials and tribulations we face, we develop a belief system that become indelibly imprinted upon our souls. This belief system has the power to either empower or oppress us for the entirety of our existence on this earthly plane.

Imagine, if you will, a scenario where you are presented with a simple iron. You have never encountered such an object before and have no knowledge of its properties. In your curiosity, you submerge the iron in water, only to be met with a painful electric shock. In that moment, you have unwittingly created a new principle which becomes a belief system in your mind - that this iron is of poor quality because it harmed you. However, had you been aware of the inherent law of electric conductivity within the iron, you would have understood that such an act was in violation of its inherent nature, leading to its destruction.

Similar principles apply to the development of our belief systems through personal experience. We may become experts in our chosen field, confident in the truths we have garnered through lived experience. However, without a foundation rooted in a broader understanding of the world, we may unknowingly adopt a flawed perspective that limits our potential for growth and fulfillment.

It is through these belief systems that we shape our personal philosophies, which in turn influence our interactions with others. Each individual on this Earth carries their own unique philosophy, born from the culmination of their experiences and understanding.

And if our belief system rests upon falsehoods, if the wisdom we have gained through experience is based on a lie, then our entire lives may exist in the shadows of deceit. Such a realization can be devastating, for our belief system is the cornerstone upon which we build our lives. It is from our personal philosophy that we derive our principles, and it is through these principles that we influence and impact the lives of others.

Therefore, it becomes imperative to examine the foundations of our beliefs, to question their veracity. Are they rooted in truth or mere illusions? By embarking on this introspective journey, we can ensure that our belief system aligns with reality, enabling us to live a life of authenticity and purpose.

Let us not be content with blindly accepting belief systems but instead seek to uncover the foundational principles that govern our existence. In doing so, we liberate ourselves from the shackles of ignorance and open the doors to a life guided by wisdom and foundational truth. This holds great significance because many of us consider ourselves to be experts, yet fail to recognize that much of the information we claim to be true is actually flawed. It is laced with biases, distortions, and a lack of relevance, making it far from reliable. Consequently, possessing knowledge does not guarantee accuracy, as much of what we learn may not be true. This brings us to an important point that we have been extensively educated in a distorted version of the truth, causing us to even dismiss any foundational truths when they confront us.

Also inventing our own truth without grounding it in a foundational truth is akin to embracing false knowledge, which I believe is the highest expression of unrestrictive idiocy. In effect, the gravest danger lies in believing falsehoods as truth. Consequently, the most hazardous individuals are those who possess strong convictions based on erroneous beliefs. History is replete with tragic examples of zealous, misguided souls whose actions have had far-reaching consequences. Such individuals possessed knowledge that, though flawed, they strongly believed to be right. Their zeal led them down a treacherous path, causing immense suffering and upheaval for humanity. Ultimately, these zealous individuals and their misguided beliefs lie at the root of many of our past and present problems. It is imperative, therefore, that we anchor our understanding and convictions in the bedrock of foundational truth to avoid falling into the dangerous trap of false knowledge.

In the same manner, the true nature of our existence and the vastness of the universe serve as constant reminders of our limitations in understanding. Scientific discoveries serve as humbling reminders of our ignorance, as each new discovery highlights something we did not previously know. Sometimes, science can become overly impressed with itself and falsely believe that it knows more than it actually does. However, the truth is that our knowledge is limited to what we have learned, and there is always more to learn. No matter how much knowledge we acquire, there will always be something we do not know. This is why it is impossible for anyone to truly know everything.

Similarly, many of us are guilty of collecting books without actually reading or fully absorbing their contents. Our libraries hold knowledge that surpasses our own, and we are faced with a sense of inadequacy whenever we look at our untouched books. We are essentially living with a fraction of the knowledge and information that life has to offer. This reality means that as humans, we all exist in a state of ignorance, where the unknown outweighs the known. Our limitations should caution us against assuming that we have full understanding or knowledge of everything.

It is a fallacy for a person to believe that they know everything. The moment someone assumes they know everything, they inadvertently reveal their own ignorance. This misconception is one of the most profound misunderstandings that humans can have. Therefore, I submit to all of us that the highest form of expression of ignorance and unrestrictive idiocy is in believing that one knows and understands everything.

From where did you form your self-definition?

The most misunderstood and toughest question that exists in the spirit of all humans is "who am I?" It is misunderstood because we miss the substance and focus only on the semantics of the question. It is also the toughest question because the answer always elicits a reaction, thus, all hell will break loose if the answer does not align with the cultural norms you were brought up in.

"Who are you?" "I am wealthy," "I am rich," "I am poor," "I am broke," "I am an HIV/AIDS patient," "I am a prisoner," "I am a student, "I am an addict," or maybe you are something else. Notice the question is "who are you?" I did not inquire about the condition of your life. If you derive your answer from your present condition, then you have not truly encountered yourself yet, as conditions can change in the blink of an eye. So, never tie who you are to your present condition because it merely reflects the state of your life, not necessarily the essence of your being.

"Who are you?" "I am a Ghanaian because I am from Africa," "I am a Chinese because I am from Asia," "I am a German because I am from Europe," "I am an American because I am from North America," "I am a Brazilian because I am from South America," "I am an Australian because I am from Australia", and what have you. By reducing "who you are" to a continent or nation, you expose the truth that you're a stranger to yourself. You may even go further, down to the city, town, village, ethnicity, or tribe your physical body originated from, and thereby strongly identify with those roots. While it is a fact of who you are, it is not the truth of who you are. Never confuse the two; know the truth of who you are.

"Who are you?" "I am a Confucianist," "I am Jain," "I am Shintoist," "I am Taoist," "I am Sikh," "I am Buddhist," "I am Hindu," "I am Jewish," "I am Muslim," "I am Christian," and more. Perhaps, you've just exposed to the world your ethical and moral conscience, indicating things you value and hold in high esteem, refusing to compromise on them for any alternative as they have become the principles of your life and the standards you live by. However, you still have not answered the question of who you are yet.

"Who are you?" "I am good," "I am fine," "I am highly favored," "I am blessed," "I am weak," "I am strong," "I am brilliant," "I am a failure," "I am unemployed," and more of that. Notice again that the question was not about how you are or what you are currently experiencing or anticipating to experience. You did not just give a wrong answer, but you also posed an illigal answer by trying to tie up who you are with how you are, what you are experiencing or anticipating. If you truly encounter yourself, you will realize that how you are, what you are experiencing or anticipating has nothing to do with the quality of your being.

"Who are you?" "I am a Prophet," "I am a teacher," "I am a lawyer," "I am a business person," "I am a politician," "I am an activist," "I am a trader," "I am a scientist," "I am a musician," "I am a footballer," "I am a King," "I am president," and many more you can list. But the real substance here is, can you identify yourself in front of others who are also doing the same? Because you simply stated what you are doing with your life, not what your life is.

My question is, is what you are doing who you really are, or did you inherit it, were you trained to become that, or was it simply passed or forced on you? If both your presence and absence cannot be felt among your colleagues who are also doing the same, then you have not really found your identity, and therefore others cannot identify your presence when you are present or even feel your absence when you are absent.

"Who are you?" "I am Jones," "I am Santos," "I am García," "I am Mbeki," "I am Yamamoto," "I am Rossi," "I am Akua," "I am Kofi." That is all well and good, but this question is not just about your name. When you delve into different cultural backgrounds, like ancient Hebrew, a person's or thing's name is deeply tied to their essence. Take Moses, for instance. In Hebrew, it means "to draw out" or "to pull out through the waters." That is why, biblically, it is said that he was drawn from the waters of the River Nile and chosen by God to lead the Israelites out of oppression in Egypt, through the Red Sea, and into the wilderness by the River Jordan. Similarly, in Hebrew, Jesus means "to deliver" or "to save." That is why biblically, He stated His purpose was not to condemn the world but to save it from the grip of sin and death, as it was already condemned.

I am left wondering, who are you really? Are you truly your given name? Do you embody the essence of your name in your daily life, or is it just a label? Perhaps you have not fully grasped the significance of your name yet. Now is the time to explore, as you might just be your name.

PRINCIPLES WORTH REMEMBERING

1. If our belief system rests upon falsehoods, if the wisdom we have gained through experience is based on a lie, then our entire lives may exist in the shadows of deceit. Such a realization can be devastating, for our belief system is the cornerstone upon which we build our lives. It is from our personal philosophy that we derive our principles, and it is through these principles that we influence and impact the lives of others.

2. It is a fallacy for a person to believe that they know everything. The moment someone assumes they know everything, they inadvertently reveal their own ignorance. This misconception is one of the most profound misunderstandings that humans can have. Therefore, I submit to all of us that the highest form of expression of ignorance and unrestrictive idiocy is in believing that one knows and understands everything.

CHAPTER

4

Unleash the Person Trapped Within You

"God made the illusion look real and the real an illusion."—Rumi

The greatest mediocrity is a product of our own systematic thinking. We are reluctant to discuss it, as we fear our illusions about our systematic approach will be exposed. We are unwilling to acknowledge that our rigid thinking has trapped us in the vicious cycle of the rat race.

So, we have refined the illusion of "systematic thinking" into a sophisticated concept called "culture". While many people believe culture is tied to a specific land, it is, in fact, a product of the people. Culture is defined by the collective systematic thinking of a community. We have conditioned ourselves to connect with one another, both spiritually and physically, and to live in harmony based on shared cultural values. We reinforce this with phrases like "Be cooperative", "Be submissive", "Don't try to be different because you are one of us", "Don't act like you know better than us, because we are the ones who nurtured you", "Who do you think you are?", "Be realistic", and more of these.

In 1943, Abraham Maslow introduced a groundbreaking theory based on his studies of the collective systematic thinking of human society, encompassing people from all walks of life. His theory revealed that, regardless of culture or time, humans are wired to think, act, and grow in a specific way, with no one exempt. In essence, we are all products of our own culture, which motivates us to wake up every day and drives our actions. This theory, known as the "Hierarchy of Needs," suggests that we must start with the most basic needs before progressing to higher-level ones. This is how we have conditioned ourselves to find out who we really are, and in the process, we are cloaked at one level or another, and we die without knowing the selves that we carry within ourselves. Let us explore how our culture has taught us to discover who we really are.

How our culture teaches us to Find who we are

I would like us to examine how we have conditioned ourselves to find who we really are, since the fall of humanity from its rightful place of dominion into the depths of ignorance, where what we do not know far outweighs what we do know. Abraham Maslow has greatly helped us with this by encapsulating these thoughts into five hierarchical needs. Let us examine this for ourselves:

- **Step 1:** *Finding ourselves through fulfilling our basic or physiological needs.*

Abraham Maslow suggests that the first step our culture teaches us to find ourselves is by fulfilling our basic or physiological needs. This starts with feeding our appetites, including food, drink, and sex, followed by seeking shelter, clothing, warmth, and sleep. It is no wonder that someone who struggles to feed their appetite may see themselves as "I am poor" and, conversely, someone who can satisfy their needs may see themselves as "I am rich" or "I am wealthy". Similarly, someone denied sex may feel unloved, unappreciated, or uncared for. If someone struggles to afford basic necessities like clothing, shelter, and warmth, they may see themselves as "I am needy". On the other hand, someone who has these necessities readily available may feel "I am lucky" or even superior to others who are struggling. This is why we spend our lives trying to tie our self-definition to these basic needs, often going to extremes like killing others just to wear a certain brand of clothing or live in a particular shelter. We exhaust ourselves daily to be seen as rich, wealthy, or good enough. Even religious beliefs perpetuate this idea, as evident in our daily prayers, which often focus on basic needs. The truth is, we have all become victims of our culture.

- **Step 2:** *Finding ourselves through safety needs.*

Finding ourselves through safety needs is the next level that all of us humans cannot escape after graduating from our basic needs. This is the level where we desire to control our circumstances, stabilise our emotions, and live our lives without interruptions or interference without our prior permission. Our ultimate desire here is to sustain, maintain, and even multiply whatever we have achieved from our basic needs. We definitely do not want to fall back to square one, and this is exactly where the spirit of hoarding comes upon us. This is where the average human, still struggling to be fulfilled at the basic level, thinks the world has robbed them of their basic needs, and they begin to break out on the streets, attacking individuals and looting resources from houses, garages, offices, and restaurants. Most of these individuals end up in jail, and we label them prisoners, convicts, and so on. That is why I am greatly influenced by Abraham Maslow's theory, because it is still realistic and relevant in our fast-changing world.

- **Step 3: *Finding ourselves through belonging.***

This level of belonging is where most of us end up after frustrating ourselves on a long run. Here is where we strive hard to get into the elite group of people's cycle. This is where we seek acceptance, building trust, friendships, and intimate relationships. We want others to reciprocate the affection and love we give to them. Here is where we literally inherit almost our belief system about our self-definition because we do all we can to fit into the circus of the majority and those of influence, becoming trapped by their self-definition of us because they clone us with who they are.

Our religious organizations, social clubs, family, and friends influence our self-definition to the extreme that we do not realize we have been cloned by them, wasting who we are. They tell you your voice sounds like this great artist, so they try to make you one, ending up washing away the self you carry inside of you. They say you act and speak like this public speaker, and immediately you try to copy everything about that person, not knowing that you are an original version. They tell you since the establishment of this world, this is the religion we have inherited, which we believe to be true, but truthfully speaking, it does not allow you to have an encounter with yourself because it tries to suffocate you with ritualistic practices, and you cannot even speak up because you know you will be seen as a rebel. They will withdraw their support from your life or even try to ignore your existence totally and even try to kill you simply because what they say is true does not make you true; it makes you wear other selves.

Our social clubs suffocate us with activities that do not make us come alive at the frontier of life; they bury who we are in their social context. Our family asks us what we see ourselves becoming, and when we tell them, if it does not strengthen their opinions about us, they try to attack us with all kinds of advice, saying something like "get this foolishness out of your head and be realistic; you cannot even feed yourself three times daily, and you're dreaming of impacting the whole world." They laugh us to death, so by the time you are grown up, you are afraid to share your dreams even with your friends and talk about yourself to people; you only talk about other people to feel important and want to become like them, which is exactly what they approve of and want you to be. Once you talk about yourself, all hell breaks loose; they put up advice in front of your eyes, which you know they are sincerely ignorant of, they try to define you by the grades on your results slips, measure you by what you cannot do, shake their heads and say do not be daydreaming, be realistic, rebuke you with sophisticated intellectual reasons why you are not that kind of person to make it impossible. And let me say to you, these people are some of the most amazing people in our lives, yet professional experts in aborting and killing who we are.

- **Step 4:** *Finding ourselves through our pursuit of self-esteem.*

This desire for self-esteem is a big deal. It is about how we see ourselves, based on what we achieve and how others see us, whether they are higher or lower than us. We strive to get power and influence, and we link our identity and value to those positions. We work hard to keep that power because we want to be noticed and respected. But many people in powerful positions cannot really define themselves; they rely on their title for identity. That is why we should not be too impressed by how they present themselves. They often do not know themselves well, just like most of us.

We also try to impress others by changing our appearance or behavior to be admired. But we do not realize that being true to ourselves is the most appealing thing. Why do we crave respect and success so much? Even if we are "holy" people, deep down, we want to be noticed and admired. But once you truly know yourself, that craving fades because authenticity is rare and attractive.

- **Step 5:** *Finally, becoming our true selves by letting go of pretences—"self-actualization."*

According to Abraham Maslow's theory, he says that after our culture pushes us through the above level of needs and we have achieved what we desire as pinpointed by our own culture in these levels of needs, then comes the final level, which is called "self-actualization." This is where we become old too soon and smart too late because we realize that all that we desire and achieve still leaves us empty; it does not integrate with ourselves, it does not align with our natural self.

That is why most successful people are not fulfilled because they have faithfully succeeded in becoming what the culture has taught them. That is why also millions of people are resigning, quitting, and changing jobs hoping to rediscover their childhood selves they carry within. Perhaps it is because they have reached a point where they realize that success is not found in achieving things but in finding fulfillment in your human spirit through the things you do.

Go out there and delve into thousands of companies, interviewing the successful employees to see if they ever personally thought about becoming what they are, and I guarantee ninety-nine percent will tell you they were influenced by somebody's teachings or were threatened that if they did not become that person, no support would be given to them when they were young.

That is why every truly successful person has a story to tell. Why? Because they went against their own cultural machinery and refused to be cloned into what people perceive them to be. These are the very people we used to call "rebels," "mad," "stubborn," "nothing," "useless," "too knowing," "demon-possessed," and now we call them "success," "heroes," "legends," and more, with higher names of respect. The truth is, the average population of the human race does not reach this level to finally discover themselves, so they end up suffocated by the content of the lower levels of need and die without knowing who they are and the lives they were meant to live. Isn't it unfair that this is how we have conditioned ourselves to find who we are, resulting in ninety-nine percent of us dying without knowing who we truly are?

Seek first to know thyself, and all other things that you desire will be attracted to you without your pursuit

All that you are seeking for in life is already in existence, waiting for you to embrace it. The paradox is you do not have to seek it first; seek the thyself trapped within yourself first, and all other things you need in life will be attracted to you. This is a natural law, and it is also biblical, as stated in Proverbs 18:16: *"A gift opens the way for the giver and ushers him into the presence of the great."*

Since we function according to natural laws, the natural law states that we must start from the bottom and work our way up. Thus, begin by seeking to know yourself first (knowing Thyself), then you will earn people's attention, recognition, admiration, and respect because you are so true to yourself that there is no falsehood in who you are. This will lead to being attracted to people and naturally drawing others to follow your lead, which is what they call "belonging". Next, you will step into safety needs, where you would not even need to seek it because people will fight to protect your reputation, what you have built and earned for yourself, because the truth is that it benefits them too - our gifts are not just for ourselves, we owe it to others to share them. Finally, you will reach basic or physiological needs, where others will compensate you for being yourself, for being original, and will go to great lengths to access the gift you carry inside, and will pay you for it with their resources. Isn't it amazing how following the natural law allows you to be natural?

The thyself that you carry within you is simply what we call a "gift." Who you really are is the question about the gift you carry on the inside of you, which you were meant to deliver to humanity before you take your final breath, and it is this gift that gives you a unique identity in this world. Let me show you what the above scripture verse really means, according to natural law, which coincides with the scriptures in truth and precision. It says there is a market out there waiting to submit their time, energy, and resources to get your gift. It says there is already an audience waiting for you to serve them with your gift, to which they will pay you for just serving. It also says your gift gets people's attention, respect, admiration, and attracts them to you. That is why you should not seek for things at the expense of yourself.

If you really want to live beyond your graveyard and your generation, find the gift you were meant to serve to the world, then become a slave to it and serve it to people. Once you find the gift you carry within you, you automatically discover who you are. I wonder what is trapped within you, just like there is flight trapped in every bird, swim in every fish, forest of trees in every seed. A seed is not really a seed; that is a fact. And what is a fact? A fact is the present description of the state of a thing. And what is the truth? It is a forest of trees, thus what it really is. So next time you have a mango seed in your palm, the truth is you are having an entire forest of trees in your palm, but the fact is, it is just a seed. Never once in your life confuse facts with truths. A fact is the description of the present state of a thing, and truth is what really a thing is. Let me guide you through the next chapter, where you will have your first-ever encounter with the truth about yourself.

PRINCIPLES WORTH REMEMBERING

1. The greatest mediocrity is a product of our own systematic thinking. We are reluctant to discuss it, as we fear our illusions about our systematic approach will be exposed. We are unwilling to acknowledge that our rigid thinking has trapped us in the vicious cycle of the rat race.

2. Our religious organizations, social clubs, family, and friends influence our self-definition to the extreme that we do not realize we have been cloned by them, wasting who we are. They tell you your voice sounds like this great artist, so they try to make you one, ending up washing away the self you carry inside of you. They say you act and speak like this public speaker, and immediately you try to copy everything about that person, not knowing that you are an original version. They tell you since the establishment of this world, this is the religion we have inherited, which we believe to be true, but truthfully speaking, it does not allow you to have an encounter with yourself because it tries to suffocate you with ritualistic practices, and you cannot even speak up because you know you will be seen as a rebel. They will withdraw their support from your life or even try to ignore your existence totally and even try to kill you simply because what they say is true does not make you true; it makes you wear other selves.

3. Our social clubs suffocate us with activities that do not make us come alive at the frontier of life; they bury who we are in their social context. Our family asks us what we see ourselves becoming, and when we tell them, if it does not strengthen their opinions about us, they try to attack us with all kinds of advice, saying something like "get this foolishness out of your

head and be realistic; you cannot even feed yourself three times daily, and you're dreaming of impacting the whole world." They laugh us to death, so by the time you are grown up, you are afraid to share your dreams even with your friends and talk about yourself to people; you only talk about other people to feel important and want to become like them, which is exactly what they approve of and want you to be. Once you talk about yourself, all hell breaks loose; they put up advice in front of your eyes, which you know they are sincerely ignorant of, they try to define you by the grades on your results slips, measure you by what you cannot do, shake their heads and say do not be daydreaming, be realistic, rebuke you with sophisticated intellectual reasons why you are not that kind of person to make it impossible. And let me say to you, these people are some of the most amazing people in our lives, yet professional experts in aborting and killing who we are.

4. Most successful people are not fulfilled because they have faithfully succeeded in becoming what the culture has taught them. That is why also millions of people are resigning, quitting, and changing jobs hoping to rediscover their childhood selves they carry within. Perhaps it is because they have reached a point where they realize that success is not found in achieving things but in finding fulfillment in your human spirit through the things you do.

5. Every truly successful person has a story to tell. Why? Because they went against their own cultural machinery and refused to be cloned into what people perceive them to be. These are the very people we used to call "rebels," "mad," "stubborn," "nothing," "useless," "too knowing," "demon-possessed," and now we call them "success," "heroes," "legends," and more, with higher names of respect.

6. All that you are seeking for in life is already in existence, waiting

for you to embrace it. The paradox is you do not have to seek it first; seek the thyself trapped within yourself first, and all other things you need in life will be attracted to you.

CHAPTER

5

The Truth About You

"Never depend on the admiration of others. There is no strength in it. Personal merit cannot be derived from an external source."—Epictetus

"The true profession of a man is to find his way to himself."
—Hermann Hesse

You came to Earth because a higher power sent you here with something important for us. Think of yourself as a special delivery sent to make this world better than before. You owe us what you carry on the inside of you, and you are obligated to share what you are carrying with us. Remember, you did not come here just for yourself, and what you have trapped on the inside of you is not just for you either. If you do not discover your inherent gift and share it with us, you are essentially stealing from this and succeeding generations because you are not letting us benefit from who you really are. It is not complicated; it is a simple idea found in nature and in biblical texts:

> *Then God said, "Let the earth bring forth grass, the herb that yields seed, and the fruit tree that yields fruit according to its kind, **whose seed is in itself, on the earth"**; and it was so. And the earth brought forth grass, the herb that yields seed according to its kind, and the tree that yields fruit, **whose seed is in itself according to its kind.** And God saw that it was good" (Genesis 1:11-12).*

According to nature and the Bible, when God created you, He packaged you. You came with everything you are supposed to become inside of you—"whose seed is in itself." God gave you everything you need to be who you are meant to be. It is like a seed inside you, waiting to become a tree. That is, according to nature, it is called a gift, and the world calls it the future or a dream.

This gift is inherent; who you really are, and no one else can give it to you. No one can lay their hands on you and give you that. No prophecy can give you that; they can only help bring it out. Your dream is not something far away; it is already within you, waiting to be unlocked. Your future is not ahead of you. It is trapped within you, striving to be released, struggling under a culture that does not believe in you.

No one can give you a future. No one can give you a dream. No one can give you a gift; they can only nurture it for you, refine it for you, and ignite it within you. Your gift is who you are and what you were born to become. And what you were born to become can never be changed. You can suffocate it with a promising career, pleasures of life, meeting the expectations of your parents or family or loved ones, or whatever else; you can even take it to the cemetery, but it can never be changed.

FIVE (5) self-expository questions for your first-ever encounter with yourself

Start by reflecting on your past, present, and future in a dedicated meeting with yourself. Take the time to answer questions related to these aspects of your life. Use a notebook, diary, computer, or any written medium that you would not easily misplace or damage. Keep in mind that these questions are interconnected, and your answers should align. If you notice they appears completely different from each other altogether, invest ample time in refining them until you are deeply convinced of each answer.

Prioritize questions with clear answers, refining those that seem less distinct as you go along. Be prepared for doubt, as some answers may challenge your existing beliefs, evoke fear, or surpass others' expectations of you. Embrace the possibility that your journey to becoming who you really are may unravel old perceptions and confront aspects of yourself you have tried to avoid. What you thought you were not might clash with the real self emerging in your awareness.

Do not be surprised if your newfound understanding challenges preconceived notions about yourself. And at the end of it all, you have to be able to reduce all the responses to a word, or a phrase, or a sentence—thus, you should be able to simplify your entire life on this planet Earth to concide with the phrase "I am... [then you fill in the blank]. This process is a gateway to re-discovering God's gift trapped within you to which you were born to deliver to this world. Embrace the discomfort, as it is part of the journey toward encountering your real self. Now, embark on this journey to meet real self for the first time.

1. What was your first thought on what you wanted to be?

This question is not as simple as we think, because we have been conditioned to prioritise what we can do over what we want to do - and this may seem acceptable, but it is a result of our culture's emphasis on mediocrity. We have forgotten that what we wanted to do is equal to our inherent potential. What we can do, in a narrow sense, is often dictated by others. The system, including our educational system, does not encourage us to pursue our dreams; instead, it constrains us with grades and reinforces the belief that what we want to do is not equal to what we can do. Friend, what did you first think of becoming before someone interfered and told you to focus on economic potential, and pursue a honourable, well-paying, and award-winning career? What was your childhood dream? What did you dream of doing when you were twelve? Be honest with yourself - what did you want to become at eighteen, and are you still pursuing that dream? If not, go back and pick up your childhood dream. That is who you truly are. If what you are now is not what you dreamed, then what you are is not natural, and that is why you may feel unfulfilled despite your achievements. Until you embrace what comes naturally to you, you will remain unfulfilled, and merely a slave to economic potential, forcing yourself to fit in and be like others who seem successful.

2. What did you love to do for fun that you dreamed of turning into into a career or profession?

If the person you dream of becoming and what you dream of doing does not stir up enthusiasm and passion in you, then you are automatically working your way towards a life without purpose. Whatever you love doing will conflict with whatever does not make you come alive naturally. This means it will frustrate you until you return to it and commit to doing it, because it literally and naturally would not make you happy doing anything else. That means you cannot change who you were born to be and become; until you embrace it, it will always frustrate you. Friend, what is that thing you love doing that does not make you feel depressed on Monday mornings and stir up excitement in you after days off, because it finally releases you from the burden of pretending to be someone else? Friend, what you love becoming and doing is exactly who you are; go and pick up yourself again.

3. What image of yourself persists in your mind, refusing to go away?

The image of yourself that sticks in your mind and would not go away is the real you! If it was not really you, it would have disappeared by now and stopped appearing in your thoughts. If it was not, you would have got rid of it by now. It keeps coming up in your mind because it is who you truly are, even when you are busy or working hard. That persistent image of yourself is the genuine you. Document it down and own your real self back, because God would not keep bringing it to mind if it was not meant to be. This is the exact you that contributes to the welfare of the world, not the one seeking welfare from the world.

4. What passion of yours is being suffocated?

Your passion is that intuition, it is the inner person within you, it is self-care and mindfulness towards others and things around you, it is the true potential you carry buried within you, it is that deep interest, enthusiasm, that thing that truly excites and generates internal motivation, commitment to making things right, to what should and could be, that artistic expression, or that creative spark within you that is being suppressed or smothered. You can always tell who you are by your passion, which is being suffocated to the extent that the inner person within you cannot breathe, grow, and be fulfilled. What is that passion when, being suffocated, it does not allow you to be yourself? That passion is the real you; it is what makes you fulfilled deep in your spirit; it is what makes you be at peace with yourself and everyone when you are being and doing that.

5. What have you found more important than seeking validation from the crowd that you want to serve to them?

It is about that sense of personal obligation to the world that you have found, rather than simply sucking up oxygen, feeding your appetite, and seeking approval. It is about the thing you have found that you will not only live for but also die for, because it is worth it. What is the thing that you have found, which you are nurturing (need to nurture) and serving (serve) to the world, even if it means potentially going against the world's expectations or opinions? It is about what matters to you most, which you want to share and distribute with others so they can experience it.

What is that sense of responsibility that lies silently in your spirit towards the world? Note that, according to natural laws, your responsibility is equal to your inherent ability or potential, which is your gift. God would not have allowed you to sense this kind of responsibility if He had not built that inherent ability within you to fulfill it. Your responsibility is equal to your ability, and your ability was built within you because there is a need or problem that you need to respond to, which made your birth and existence necessary. What is that sense of responsibility silently crying out from within you, even if you try to suffocate it? Once you discover your responsibility towards the world, you simultaneously discover your inherent ability, which is the gift you carry within you, and you owe it to the crowd that you were born to deliver it to them before you take your final breath on this planet Earth.

"Above all, don't lie to yourself."—Fyodor Dostoevsky

PRINCIPLES WORTH REMEMBERING

1. You came to Earth because a higher power sent you here with something important for us. Think of yourself as a special delivery sent to make this world better than before. You owe us what you carry on the inside of you, and you are obligated to share what you are carrying with us. Remember, you did not come here just for yourself, and what you have trapped on the inside of you is not just for you either. If you do not discover your inherent gift and share it with us, you are essentially stealing from this and succeeding generations because you are not letting us benefit from who you really are.

2. When God created you, He packaged you. You came with everything you are supposed to become inside of you—"whose seed is in itself." God gave you everything you need to be who you are meant to be. It is like a seed inside you, waiting to become a tree. That is, according to nature, it is called a gift, and the world calls it the future or a dream. This gift is inherent; who you really are, and no one else can give it to you. No one can lay their hands on you and give you that. No prophecy can give you that; they can only help bring it out. Your dream is not something far away; it is already within you, waiting to be unlocked. Your future is not ahead of you. It is trapped within you, striving to be released, struggling under a culture that does not believe in you.

3. No one can give you a future. No one can give you a dream. No one can give you a gift; they can only nurture it for you, refine

it for you, and ignite it within you. Your gift is who you are and what you were born to become. And what you were born to become can never be changed. You can suffocate it with a promising career, pleasures of life, meeting the expectations of your parents or family or loved ones, or whatever else; you can even take it to the cemetery, but it can never be changed.

4. We have been conditioned to prioritise what we can do over what we want to do - and this may seem acceptable, but it is a result of our culture's emphasis on mediocrity. We have forgotten that what we wanted to do is equal to our inherent potential. What we can do, in a narrow sense, is often dictated by others. The system, including our educational system, does not encourage us to pursue our dreams; instead, it constrains us with grades and reinforces the belief that what we want to do is not equal to what we can do.

5. If the person you dream of becoming and what you dream of doing does not stir up enthusiasm and passion in you, then you are automatically working your way towards a life without purpose. Whatever you love doing will conflict with whatever does not make you come alive naturally. This means it will frustrate you until you return to it and commit to doing it, because it literally and naturally would not make you happy doing anything else. That means you cannot change who you were born to be and become; until you embrace it, it will always frustrate you.

6. Your passion is that intuition, it is the inner person within you, it is self-care and mindfulness towards others and things around you, it is the true potential you carry buried within you, it is that deep interest, enthusiasm, that thing that truly excites and generates internal motivation, commitment to making things right, to what should and could be, that artistic expression, or that creative spark within you that is being suppressed or

smothered. You can always tell who you are by your passion, which is being suffocated to the extent that the inner person within you cannot breathe, grow, and be fulfilled.

7. According to natural laws, your responsibility is equal to your inherent ability or potential, which is your gift. God would not have allowed you to sense this kind of responsibility if He had not built that inherent ability within you to fulfill it. Your responsibility is equal to your ability, and your ability was built within you because there is a need or problem that you need to respond to, which made your birth and existence necessary. Once you discover your responsibility towards the world, you simultaneously discover your inherent ability, which is the gift you carry within you, and you owe it to the crowd that you were born to deliver it to them before you take your final breath on this planet Earth.

Chapter

6

Living Beyond Yourself

"We are reduced to asking others what we are. We never dare to ask ourselves."—JJ Rousseau

You are a package of value to this world. And if you never deliver that package to the world, you are a professional generational thief. Also, if you ever submit your life to destruction, fleeting pleasures, or suicide, you are the greatest curse to have come upon the surface of this planet Earth, because you are not giving anything back to the betterment of this world; you are only making it more bitter than it was before you ever existed.

Friend, in order to become valuable to us, humanity, and live your life beyond the graveyard to affect succeeding generations, you are then obligated to become a servant to the gift, future, or dream you have found within you, nurture it, refine it, and serve it to the world. That is the only way you can live beyond yourself, thus making your absence felt after you have taken your last breath.

But here is a big one: the person you have discovered trapped within you, no one can see; you are the only one who can see it. For others to see it, unless it is revealed to them by God, the Creator of all things from Heaven to them. Let us take a biblical case study of why we greatly misunderstood Jesus Christ.

In Chapter 16 of the book of Matthew in the Bible, Jesus asked a question that most of us would not dare because our culture discourages us from talking about ourselves and instead encourages us to focus on becoming like others. Moreover, our culture shapes our identity, so asking such questions invites criticism and attack. Yet Jesus, who had transcended cultural norms, asked His disciples, *"Who do people say the Son of Man is?" (Matthew 16:13).* Their responses mirrored what modern minds might say: *"Some say John the Baptist; others say Elijah; and still others, Jeremiah or one of the prophets" (Matthew 16:14).* In other words, unable to fully comprehend Him, they reduced Him to a prophet. This prompts me to wonder, in your cultural context, how have others reduced you? They do not know who you really are; instead, they project their perceptions onto you, often inaccurately.

That is why, to this day, humanity has held various misconceptions about Him and who He is. Many view Him as a rebel, a misfit, and a fanatic. Some see Him as a well-intentioned but misguided rabbinical teacher whose teachings seem to challenge and contaminate the established doctrines of Moses and Judaism. Meanwhile, they have reduced Moses' profound message to a rigid religion, prioritising strict adherence to laws rather than understanding the deeper intent behind those laws. They expect Him to conform to this pattern.

For Muslims, He is perceived as a revered holy prophet in line with other holy prophets, an exceptional teacher, but ultimately falls short in delivering complete redemption for humanity. Hindus also see Him as a wise teacher and a good person, adding Him to their pantheon of deities to fulfil their spiritual needs. On the other hand, atheists, agnostics, and humanists acknowledge His historical existence but dismiss His miracles and claims of divinity, viewing Him as a human figure deified by misguided followers.

The media, scientists, and secularists consider Him a subject for analysis, debate, and criticism, often ignoring His divine assertions and questioning His validity and existence. Christians, despite their faith, sometimes misunderstand Him, reducing His teachings to mere rituals and His promises as a means to achieve personal gain or escape from hell's torment.

The crux lies in His non-religious essence. He never adhered to any established religion during His time. He did not align with religion in His time like the Pharisees, Sadducees, or Herodians, nor did He partake in religious councils or rituals. Surprisingly, His primary opposition stemmed from religious circles rather than sinners. His identity transcended the religious paradigm, which unsettled the established order. Contrary to popular belief, He did not introduce a religion; instead, He offered a distinct Kingdom meant for all humanity. His disruption was not about religion but about presenting a universal kingdom beyond existing religious frameworks *(Get a copy of my book, titled "Where Am I From?" - Volume 1 of "The Lost Human Factor". In this book, I talk about humanity greatest pursuit, and also why Jesus Christ is the most misunderstood person on this planet Earth in more understanding details from a broad human conviction stemming from foundational truths and their inherent principles).*

I wonder who you have been reduced to?

BECOMING WHO YOU REALLY ARE

The greatest example of how to become who you really are or deliver your gift to humanity is to imitate God's principle. "Living Beyond Yourself" is the clearest example we have, and it is what everyone on Earth is supposed to do - imitate God's principle. You were born to deliver something to Earth from God, and God has set up a prototype of how we can become our real selves or deliver our gift to humanity. Whatever God does is an example of His principle, and His principle always succeeds - even growing a seed in soil or growth medium to become a tree is full of revelation. That is why I would rather follow God's principle or strategy than a human's, because we have failed so many times, but God has never failed. The theme here is that when God does something, it succeeds, and we must copy His strategy.

To become your real self or deliver your gift to humanity, it is not a pursuit to seek; rather, it is the result of a process. Let us examine how a seed becomes its real self—a tree, which is a gift that I have sought to emulate in becoming the person I am today:

> ***Never doubt yourself:*** I have never seen a mango seed trying to become a pear tree. I have never seen a mango seed working its way out to become a cocoa tree because of the promising economic potential that it will be able to gain attention and draw much wealth from the global economy market. No matter how promising the future is when it becomes a cocoa tree, it will always tend to become itself, thus a mango tree with its mango fruits on it, and become a package of value to attract wealth at its own season, to which everybody needed it simply because it is its time. Friend, are you becoming yourself, or are you following the dictates of promising economic potential to end up falling into the dungeon of

becoming a slave to a whole machinery called employment without deploying yourself?

Becoming yourself is a monumental achievement in a world constantly pushing you to conform. Trusting yourself is key—do not yield to societal pressures that conflict with what you sees you really are in the eyes of your mind. Do not carry guilt for not meeting others' expectations; focus on nurturing your gift and deliver it to us, humanity. You are not here to follow religious or school paths forced upon you by others; embrace your authenticity.

Some people regretfully say, "I didn't want to become this." They have faced inner conflicts, conforming to societal expectations, and devaluing themselves to fit into the world's mold. But you, my friend, do not need to devalue yourself for acceptance. Be authentic; if others cannot appreciate it, move forward. You do not require validation to become who God intended you to be. Do not worry about being by doing it perfectly now; progress matters. In time, you will settle into yourself, grateful you did not conform.

> *Surround yourself with people who accept you for who you are, without trying to change you into a copy of themselves or their idea of who you should be:* You know, just being with some people is a problem because they are full of demands. They expect you to like what they like, they want you to dress and speak like them, they want you to go into the same career as them, they want you to think and act like them. In other words, they always want you to follow their lives without you leading your own. Notice that these are all good people, but they are not the right people for you. They do not want you to run your own life; they always want to run your life for you.

They push you to the edge of prioritizing their opinion above yours and who you really are. Neither will they allow you to pursue your dreams because they are like plants around you that contain allelopathic chemicals that inhibit your growth. I tell you, these people are parasites preying on your ignorance of who you really are; they are using you for their own self-interests, and you need to leave that circle of relationships and be with people who will encourage and help you with their resources to keep nurturing your dream pregnancy. These are the people who would not abort your dream because they are your right environment.

> ***Impose self-restrictions on yourself for greater acceleration of growth:*** Knowing thyself is the beginning of all your greatest achievements. Once you get to know who you really are, you will gain revelatory knowledge that some things in life are good but are not right for you. Just like a seed discovering it is really a tree, it would not under any circumstances - not even a good one - opt for phosphorus for its leaf growth or nitrogen for its root growth. Why? Because it is not right for who it is as a tree. Instead, it needs phosphorus for its root growth and nitrogen for its leaf growth, and that is exactly what is right for it. Friend, you know deep down in your human spirit that there are meetings you need to stop attending, others you need to start attending, programs you need to participate in at certain seasons in your life, and others that are not right for you - even if they are free. And there are tapes, audios, and podcasts you need to shut your eyes and ears to. Why? Because they are not the right nutrients for you; they may be perfect for others, but not you. That is why knowing thyself is important: it helps you escape errors and abuses you might inevitably inflict on

your gift, dream, or future. Once you know thyself, you need no one to tell you which field of study you should pursue in school or which career you should choose. Knowing thyself is the beginning of liberation from your cultural environment, which wants to clone you with other selves. Even knowing thyself helps you discern which food is right for your body system or not, what kind of people you should associate with or allow into your circle, which social or religious club memberships you need to give up on, and what dresses you should wear. That is the power of knowing the person trapped inside you, who is obligated to release their package of value to us, humanity.

> ***Refine your gift for excellence:*** No man wants to eat an unripe banana or take a squeeze of juice from an unripe mango or orange, unless it is ripe. Notice that when it has ripened, it does not go looking for a market; it is rather attracted to the market, and people come for it at exactly the spot it was planted and has grown to become itself, with its fruit on it. That's the same thing that happens to our gift. If, after discovering who we really are, we don't pursue becoming an expert in who we really are and refine our gifts for excellence, to their best quality standard, we would not be valuable to humanity, although our value will still be there and remain undepreciated. If we do not become the best quality and version of ourselves, our value is still wrapped up, and no one will see it.

Let me give you a Bible quote from Proverbs 22:29, which says, *"Observe people who are good at their work - skilled workers are always in demand and admired; they don't take a back seat to anyone."* The root word for the word "work" here is "eregon", which means "to be" or "to become", and the skill here means best quality, version, or standard. That exactly means that only those who are the best version of themselves, nurture and serve their gifts at their finest, high quality are those who are always in demand and admired, why? Because they are being noticed, the world makes room for them, so they are not at the back seat to anyone.

I like the NIV version better because it is contemporary in its rendition; it goes like this: *"Do you see a man skilled in his work? He will serve before kings; he will not serve before obscure men."* In other words, you will know you have refined your gift to the highest quality and standard when you are serving it before kings; the Bible explains this further, saying that you will not serve it before the "obscure", that is unknown or infamous people. To put it further, if who, or the market, or the audience you are serving your gift to is not known in the world, then your gift is unknown in the world, and if it is unknown, there will be no demand upon your life for it.

That is why from this moment forward, you must decide to become your own school to educate yourself, because no one can nurture your gift on the inside of you to the best quality, standard, and version as God intended for you. Train, listen to good tapes, watch good programs, read good books, get a mentor, and submit yourself to help you save yourself from five years of mistakes you will make in the area of your gifting. Attend seminars that will fertilize your dreams, build high-quality relationships that will expand your root system to reach out for more nutrients to stimulate your dream, and join associations that will water and throw sunlight on you to reach the best version of yourself. This is important because a gift that has been refined to excellence attracts more demands on it. That is to tell, regardless of your location on this planet, refining your gift to excellence will attract global attention, and people will go to great lengths - literally traveling by air, water, or land - to access your exceptional gift.

> ***Make yourself adaptable to global changes:*** You can always determine the quality you need to improve in your gifting based on the world's needs. Just like a plant breeder can sense and develop a new variety of watermelon based on the needs of the market; whether it ismaking it resilient and resistant to diseases, draught, heat stress, or it seedless or changing its circular shape to a heart shape, square shape, or any shape at all, based on the demand for it. You, too, need the same revelatory knowledge so that you will be responsive to global needs, and God has built into you the ability to meet those needs. Always keep your eyes on what the people you're serving your gift to are looking for. Here's the key: any need you identify, you have the inherent ability to fulfill it.

> ***Be a slave to your gift:*** You owe a debt to us, humanity. And you are responsible for paying that debt to us, by using the gift you carry inside your human spirit. You are obligated to deliver and serve us with your gift. Your value to us comes from serving your gift to us, and that is exactly what made your birth necessary and your existence important to us.

The most perfect person and greatest leader who ever walked upon the surface of this planet Earth said these words, *"For even I, the Son of Man, came here not to be served but to serve others, and to give my life as a ransom for many"* (Mark 10:45). Jesus Christ understood His reason for existence on this planet, and He knew that He did not come to Earth for Himself but for us, humanity, and that the debt He owes us is eternal life. So, He came to this planet Earth to pay that debt through crucifixion on the cross, with blood and sweat running all over His body from the wounds and pores on His skin that were inflicted upon Him because of our sins. And now, those who turn to Him, as He is the true Vine and eat from His fruit, which is the gift of eternal life, now have the nutrient of eternal life. We have both life and death insurance; we are fully covered from the sting of sin and death. That is why an untold number of people still turn to Jesus Christ up to date because He is the only person in the history of humanity who has the gift of eternal life and is the way to the truth.

I wonder, if Jesus Christ had not discovered who He really was and delivered His gift of eternal life to us, He would have robbed us of resurrection; life after death, and humanity would have been in a mess forever. There is a gift you are carrying within you, which humanity needs to function properly and to live effectively; do not rob us of your gift.

Here is my point: the gift is more important than the person. Your gift is so powerful that your enemies will come to you and pay you for it. Your gift is so powerful it attracts people to it, not to you, because they may even not like you. People will walk over their pride and come to you for it. And also, if your gift is supplying someone, they will make sure that you are personally secured and maintained in the history of humanity.

Friend, be a slave to your gift, nurture it, refine it, and serve it to us. That is how you become valuable, a great person, and a legend to us. And I guarantee you, at the point you cease living in your physical body, you would not need any tombstone to mark a spot here on this planet that you too existed on Earth because your life was too useful to us that you have literally etched yourself in our history, and we cannot forget you, and so we do not need to visit your graveyard to remind ourselves that you used to be part of us. Why? Because you are living beyond yourself in the graveyard.

PRINCIPLES WORTH REMEMBERING

1. You are a package of value to this world. And if you never deliver that package to the world, you are a professional generational thief. Also, if you ever submit your life to destruction, fleeting pleasures, or suicide, you are the greatest curse to have come upon the surface of this planet Earth, because you are not giving anything back to the betterment of this world; you are only making it more bitter than it was before you ever existed.

2. To become your real self or deliver your gift to humanity, it is not a pursuit to seek; rather, it is the result of a process.

3. Becoming yourself is a monumental achievement in a world constantly pushing you to conform. Trusting yourself is key—do not yield to societal pressures that conflict with what you sees you really are in the eyes of your mind. Do not carry guilt for not meeting others' expectations; focus on nurturing your gift and deliver it to us, humanity. You are not here to follow religious or school paths forced upon you by others; embrace your authenticity.

4. You know, just being with some people is a problem because they are full of demands. They expect you to like what they like, they want you to dress and speak like them, they want you to go into the same career as them, they want you to think and act like them. In other words, they always want you to follow their lives without you leading your own. Notice that these are all good people, but they are not the right people for you. They do not want you to run your own life; they always want to run your life for you. They push you to the edge of prioritizing their opinion above yours and who you really are. Neither will they allow you

to pursue your dreams because they are like plants around you that contain allelopathic chemicals that inhibit your growth. I tell you, these people are parasites preying on your ignorance of who you really are; they are using you for their own self-interests, and you need to leave that circle of relationships and be with people who will encourage and help you with their resources to keep nurturing your dream pregnancy. These are the people who would not abort your dream because they are your right environment.

5. Knowing thyself is the beginning of all your greatest achievements. Once you get to know who you really are, you will gain revelatory knowledge that some things in life are good but are not right for you. Just like a seed discovering it is really a tree, it would not under any circumstances - not even a good one - opt for phosphorus for its leaf growth or nitrogen for its root growth. Why? Because it is not right for who it is as a tree. Instead, it needs phosphorus for its root growth and nitrogen for its leaf growth, and that is exactly what is right for it.

6. You owe a debt to us, humanity. And you are responsible for paying that debt to us, by using the gift you carry inside your human spirit. You are obligated to deliver and serve us with your gift. Your value to us comes from serving your gift to us, and that is exactly what made your birth necessary and your existence important to us.

7. The gift is more important than the person. Your gift is so powerful that your enemies will come to you and pay you for it. Your gift is so powerful it attracts people to it, not to you, because they may even not like you. People will walk over their pride and come to you for it. And also, if your gift is supplying someone, they will make sure that you are personally secured and maintained in the history of humanity.

Afterword

I am much convinced that by now you should be prepared to die. In other words, to become who you were destined to be, and to which you are convicted that this is what you truly are, you must be ready to sacrifice who you are now, shaped by your cultural environment, if it is not worth being that person for all the days of your life on this planet Earth.

It is my deepest aspiration that you will deploy yourself to us before you cease living in your physical body. It is my conviction that you will deliver to us what you owe us, so that you do not become a generation thief who has robbed us of the value of your life. It is my deepest hope that you will live beyond yourself and your generation and impact us with whatever you carry within you that God sent you here to transfer to us.

To leave you with a word of caution: do not be overly impressed when people are drawn to you, because it is not about you; it is about your gift. People are really looking for what you are carrying within you; they are looking for what God has bestowed upon your life. If you confuse people's admiration, attention, and respect for you with them being attracted to you as a person, then you have really missed it; they are rather attracted to your gift, not you.

That is why I implore you to treat everybody who comes to you with a level of reverence and respect. Never think highly of yourself; be humble, regardless of who the person is, because they have walk over their pride and jealousy and come to you. So, serve them with the best version of yourself, deliver your gift to them, so that they can experience the value that is within you. Release your life to them, so that you will live beyond yourself when you are no longer part of the land of the living. I encourage you to let this be your greatest pursuit in life, because, in case you have forgotten, no one is destined to live forever - that includes you.

Copyright

© 2024 by Paa Kwasi Mfoamfo.

About the Author

Joseph Bekoe Mfoamfo, known by the pen name Paa Kwasi Mfoamfo, hails from a humble background in Larteh-Akuapem, Eastern region of Ghana, West Africa. Paa Kwasi Mfoamfo, an influential speaker, delves into fundamental issues that shape human conviction, encompassing spiritual and social dimensions. His teachings revolve around living effectively and dying satisfactory, while also addressing the prevailing moral and ethical challenges in our swiftly evolving global society. Paa Kwasi Mfoamfo's personal conviction aligns with a broader human perspective, and his vision for the world seeks to instigate positive change from a grounded, realistic, and sustainable standpoint – a place he refers to as Heaven.

Paa Kwasi Mfoamfo's impactful messages are imbued with power, serving to inspire, motivate, challenge, and empower individuals. His focus lies in prompting humanity to pause, look inward, and consider their values, choices, and impact on others and the world around them. To re-discover their true selves, unlock unused potentials, and actively contribute to their immediate surroundings and the wider global community. The ultimate goal is to encourage people to leave a lasting impact before they take their last breath on this planet Earth.

You are welcome to contact Paa Kwasi Mfoamfo directly at his personal email, **mfoamfo@gmail.com**, if you would like him to speak at your conference, anniversary, meeting, or to motivate your team. He is open to invitations from companies, organizations, associations, or any social clubs focused on enhancing the well-being of people.

Don't miss out!

Visit the website below and you can sign up to receive emails whenever Paa Kwasi Mfoamfo publishes a new book. There's no charge and no obligation.

https://books2read.com/r/B-A-QFMEB-QQHED

Connecting independent readers to independent writers.